THE
MEDITATION
BOOK

THE MEDITATION BOOK

Eddie and Debbie Shapiro

A GODSFIELD BOOK

Dedication

We are grateful to our teachers — Paramahamsa Satyananda,
Sri Swami Satchidananda, His Eminence Tai Situ Rinpoche and His Holiness
The Dalai Lama — for sharing with us their wisdom and compassion
and the joy of meditation.

First published in Great Britain in 2000 by Godsfield Press Ltd
A division of David and Charles Ltd
Brunel House, Forde Close,
Newton Abbot, Devon TQ12 4PU UK

10 9 8 7 6 5 4 3 2

© 2000 Godsfield Press
Text © 2000 Eddie and Debbie Shapiro

Designed for Godsfield Press by
The Bridgewater Book Company

Photographer *Ian Parsons*
Illustrators *Olivia Rayner, Sabine Kussmaul*, MTG
Picture researcher *Claire Gouldstone*

Manufactured in China

ISBN 1-84181-021-5

The publishers wish to thank the following for the use of pictures in this pack:

Front jacket pictures: The Stock Market. AKG: 11,16, 24, 38, 40, 70. e.t. archive: 41, 78.
Image Bank: 69 (Marc Romanelli). Images Colour Library: 94. Caroline Jones: 15, 22/23, 49.
Science Photo Library: 42. The Stock Market: 28 (Rob Matheson), 61 (S. Wilkings),
92 (Jose L. Pelaez Inc.). Tony Stone Images: 6 (David Patterson), 8/9, 71 (Michael Busselle),
13 (Art Wolfe), 18/19 (Simon McComb), 26/27 (Lori Adamski Peek), 29 (Cosmo Condina),
31 (William J. Herbert), 39, 79 (Ken Fisher), 41 (Hugh Sitton), 50/51 (Bryan Mullennix),
59 (Ian O'Leary), 64/65 (Tim Brown), 80 (David Loftus), 81 (Dan Bosler),
83 (Bob Thomason), 86 (Brian Bailey), 90 (Chris Thomaidis).
Copyright © Coral Corporation: card nos., 15–30.

contents

Introduction

The Tibetan wheel of life showing the stages of spiritual development.

Have you ever noticed how your mind seems to wander from one subject to another? Or how easily you become caught up in irrational worries or dramas? Or how you seem unable to change your behavior, even though you want to? Do you wake up feeling apprehensive about the day ahead? Do you get impatient or irritable? These are just some of the indications of a mind that is distressed, confused, and distracted. Luckily, there is an instant cure — meditation!

Meditation is a spontaneous and natural part of being human, but, because we are under stress, we fail to experience the riches of deep relaxation and inner peace that are our essential nature. Instead, we "contract" and become irritated, depressed, overwhelmed, and exhausted.

We practice meditation in order to regain our natural balance. It is simple and easy to do, and the rewards are bountiful. You will enjoy far greater peace of mind, along with the ability to focus with more clarity so you are less subject to every whim and fancy.

So that meditation can become your friend, something that you enjoy doing, we have devised this book to lead you into this art step by step. You will learn different techniques to help you find the one that suits you best, as well as how to breathe, sit comfortably, and deal with your chattering mind.

As you read this book, stop and try each technique. Meditate every day, even if you can only spare a few minutes to do so. Every moment you manage to devote to it will help you to discover for yourself the beauty of meditation. Some people will feel most comfortable when doing the breath awareness meditation, while others may prefer the loving kindness practice. In discovering exactly where your preferences lie, you will be listening to your own inner wisdom. We each have a teacher within us, when we stop to listen. Meditation connects you to your light and to the freedom to be found within.

The Daily Meditation cards included in this pack are meant to inspire and remind you of the qualities of the meditative mind. Take one and recall it throughout your day. Let it be a constant inspiration to you and remind you of the benefits of a clear mind and an open heart.

Contemplating nature can help you to discover inner peace.

What is Meditation?

Many of us experience a meditative state without realizing it — e.g., times when we are sitting outdoors, perhaps beside a stream or in a peaceful backyard, when everything seems to drop away, including all our thoughts or concerns, and we enter into a deeply peaceful stillness ... an inner quiet. In this quiet, we feel as if we have dissolved and are no longer something separate or individual, but have merged with everything around us. We become the trees, the birds, the water — there is no separation, no difference between us.

This state is very joyful; however, it does not necessarily last! Our minds and senses are so powerful that we become distracted by every-day concerns, pulled into our worries or personal dramas, our habits or confusion, until this feeling of inner quiet seems very far away. However, the more we practice meditation, i.e., specific techniques to purposefully bring the mind into a focused and still place, the more we experience an inner quiet.

The practice of meditation, which may include contemplation and prayer, is an aspect of all the great religious traditions; it is as well-known in Eastern systems as it is in Christianity. Inner stillness is seen as the route to experiencing God. If we are too externalized and busy with thoughts, we are unable to perceive the beauty around us or to receive divine inspiration. But meditation is not limited to religious practice; it also has far-reaching implications in our fast-moving and highly demanding world for bringing balance and harmony to our lives.

When they first begin meditating, many people describe feeling as if they have "come home." In entering this quiet "inner space," you connect with yourself in a more genuine way. It feels familiar, like a place you have been away from for some time. You realize how most of your time is spent being distracted, and how little you really know yourself inside.

Meditation is not a goal in itself. It is not something you try to achieve. Rather, it is an awakened way of being. The meditative mind is one that is balanced, clear, and at ease, focused entirely on what is happening in this moment, fully present and compassionate.

The purpose of practicing meditation is to bring about the transformation of our perception of ourselves and our world — from that of skepticism and doubt to acceptance and kindness — so we become more awake. This happens as stress, confusion, and mental chatter lessen, understanding deepens, and compassion and inner peacefulness emerge. But this is not something to merely read about — it is in the experience of meditation that you will find these words begin to make sense and bear fruit.

Meditation enables you to discover an abiding inner joy.

Just-being Meditation

PRACTICE PAGE

*M*editation brings you into the present moment – into being here, now. To begin your exploration of the meditative state, start with this simple practice of just being for 10–30 minutes.

⊙ Remove your shoes and find a comfortable place to sit (see page 54). Close your eyes and become aware of your breath. Just watch it as it enters and leaves your body, noting its rise and fall. Do not try to change your breath – just observe its movement.

⊙ Slowly become aware of your body ... of your feet ... where they are touching the floor ... of the floor's texture and how your feet feel upon it. Then slowly move your awareness up your legs ... sensing how they are, feeling any sensations like heat, cold or tingling, and just experience anything that arises. Follow your awareness to your buttocks ... to their contact with the chair or cushion beneath you ... and release any tension with your breath while you observe your body.

Now bring your awareness up your back, becoming aware of your spine and the muscles in your back ... Then proceed to your pelvis and abdomen ... as you breathe in and out, notice how your abdomen moves ... bring your awareness higher to your chest and to the rise and fall with each breath ... just observe ... witness your body.

Now become aware of your hands resting in your lap. Without moving them, note each finger ... your palms ... the backs of your

Chakras are symbols of the energy centers or levels of perception throughout the body.

hands ... moving up your arms ... to your shoulders ... neck and face. Sense each detail of your face ... your lips ... nose ... eyes ... ears ... and the whole of your head, including back and top.

◉ Gently come back to your breathing ... feel your body sitting on the chair or cushion ... feel the presence of your being ... the energy moving in and through you that is your essence.

As you sit observing yourself, be aware of any sounds around you ... and of your environment. Notice how you are part of your environment – not separate – and sense how you are connected to everything around you.

◉ Sit like this without moving for as long as you like ... just breathing and being ... just being here, right now, in this minute; in this moment, nothing else exists. Be the moment.

When you are ready, take a deep breath and exhale very slowly. Then open your eyes and have a good stretch, savoring the beneficial feelings this practice brings to your body and mind.

Being and observing creates composure and calmness.

Forms of Meditation

The mind is like the flame on a log — it needs something to burn or to do, and loves entertainment. By giving it a specific activity, it gradually stops jumping all over the place and begins to grow focused and quiet. This is especially so if the activity we give it is a repetitive one, such as counting the breaths or repeating a mantra, which allows the mind to focus on just one thing. It becomes one-pointed and thus calms down while developing greater balance and stability.

The flickering flame of your mind becomes still as you meditate upon a lighted candle.

There are many forms of meditation, and each one is useful in its own unique way. What is important is to find the technique that suits you best as an individual.

These various techniques may be roughly categorized as those which stimulate deep relaxation and ease; develop the mind in concentration, absorption, and stability; deepen insight and wisdom; open the heart by developing loving kindness and forgiveness; and enable us to go beyond ourselves through prayer and devotion. We have included examples of all of these in this book so that you may find the one that that is most appropriate for you.

The common factor in all forms of meditation is the attention paid to breathing. The breath connects you with your inner world, and through its rhythm, you immediately enter into a quiet space. Focusing on the breath, therefore, tends to begin each session of meditation.

To encourage deep relaxation and ease, you involve the creative mind through using visualization exercises. Using the breath to relax and focus, you then create images that are specifically healing, such as being on a deserted beach, floating in ocean waves, or walking in the countryside. Such images have a calming effect that releases deep levels of stress and tension within you. In the same way, affirmations, or positive statements, can be used to release your old self-images and to allow new ways of being to emerge.

In order to develop concentration and awareness, use the breath. Watch its *in* and *out* rhythm, or count each breath, until you become focused. You can also use a mantra – a repetitive soothing sound or phrase – to focus the mind. Or concentrate on a candle flame or image and then close your eyes and visualize it mentally.

To develop insight, simply learn to be present with yourself. Observe your thoughts and sensations, watching how they come and go, until you see beneath thoughts to the innate wisdom within yourself.

Developing qualities like loving kindness and forgiveness means opening your heart to both yourself and others. You can learn to slowly release your resistance to or dislike of others and to find a deeper level of understanding in which you accept others and yourself with compassion.

Through prayer and devotion, you reach beyond yourself to connect with the divine. You go beyond your individual self to merge with that which is greater.

Visualize an inspiring natural scene to create your own personal retreat.

Meditation as Medicine

Meditation teaches you to be more aware of your physical body.

Whenever you feel distressed or tense, there is an immediate reaction in the physical body: the digestive system begins to shut down, the heart rate increases, hormones flood the body, and the nervous system goes on red alert. If this happens too often, you start suffering from the degenerative effects of stress. For many people, it happens all too often. It may not be big problems that cause stress; more likely, small difficulties accumulate until you reach a point where you feel that you just cannot cope any more.

The word *meditation* has the same root as *medicine*, and so we can think of it as a cure for both the body and the mind. What a gift! Meditation lowers blood pressure, reduces inner tension, calms the cardiovascular and nervous systems, and strengthens the immune system. This has the immediate effect of reducing stress.

Meditation is also very helpful for releasing physical pain. When you experience pain, your normal reaction is to tense your body against it, to resist it in any way you can. However, such resistance can actually serve to increase the level of pain. Meditation shows you how to simply be with what is – how to have direct awareness of something without resisting it. This helps to soften to the pain, teaching you to let go of the tension surrounding it, so you can release it yourself. Pain then becomes a teacher, showing you where you are resisting or tightening your mind and body.

The Buddha, who was a master of meditation, described meditation as the greatest medicine for the mind – a remedy for anger, ill-will, irritation, agitation, worry, and all the other destructive mental states imaginable. Through meditation, the mind is eased and its accumulated tension released. But, more importantly, as you meditate you develop greater objectivity, and begin to see yourself and your various states of mind more clearly.

As your insight grows, you begin to see the deeper causes of your upset and just how you maintain or perpetuate destructive ways of thinking. As you sit quietly in meditation, the heat of past anger or conflict is cooled. You see that perhaps you acted without awareness of the whole situation, or that someone who was angry with you was actually harboring a deep pain in himself, and so you can extend your compassion to him.

While reflecting about the emotional roller coaster on which you can find yourself, you begin to see how, for instance, anger comes and goes in you, but that, in essence, you are not an angry person. Rather, you are really considerate, but become angry now and then. Your meditation brings the more loving part of your personality to the surface. You see your unskillful actions – i.e., those that hurt others – and can let them go with love and forgiveness. In this respect, meditation is like a balm that soothes the aches of the mind and brings healing.

Meditation enables you to find a level of inner healing and happiness that releases you from a need for external satisfaction. You find a place of confidence within you that does not depend on affirmation or praise from others. The medicine of meditation heals your doubts and insecurities, and you become more self-assured as you get to know and make friends with yourself.

The more you simplify your life, the greater your inner freedom.

Three Mini-Meditations

A mandala – a symbol of the universe used for meditation.

Meditation does not have to be practiced in a formal way for a certain amount of time while you are in a particular position. Having a structure for it definitely helps, but you can also practice meditation wherever you are, at any time. Try one of these mini-meditations for a few minutes or longer, and note how your state of mind changes, relaxing and becoming more peaceful.

SOFT BREATH

Focusing on your breathing relaxes the body and cultivates attentiveness.

Find a comfortable place to sit and close your eyes. Focus on your abdomen, take a deep breath, filling your lungs, and as you exhale, feel all of the tension inside you being released. Do this three times, repeating to yourself: *soft belly, soft belly, soft belly*. As you soften your muscles, any tension there will leave and you will relax more deeply.

Once your abdomen is relaxed, return to your normal breathing and watch your breath for a few minutes. Simply observe the flow of your breath as it enters and leaves your body.

Then shift your awareness to your heart, and watch your breath as it enters and leaves your chest, while at the same time repeating: *soft heart, soft heart, soft heart*. As you relax your heart, love and compassion will naturally arise. Then return to normal breathing when you are ready and greet your world with a smile on your face and in your heart.

16

WALKING WITHOUT ARRIVING

We normally walk without any awareness. You can do this practice any time you are walking – whether to your car, the grocery, in a park, at work. Walk at whatever speed you want – slow or fast. All you do is watch yourself walking; you walk with awareness. Notice the rise and fall of your feet, the movement in your legs and hips, and how your whole body shifts and flows. Then, coordinate your breath with the steps you take so you breathe and walk in rhythm. Do this for as long as feels comfortable. The object is to become aware of each movement you make. When you are finished, stand still for a moment before carrying on with your day.

EXTENDING LOVING KINDNESS

Our feelings about other people, and their feelings about us, have a profound influence upon all of us, for good or bad. Feelings of irritability, resentment, or upset can be eased and embraced by developing loving kindness and compassion. Achieve this by doing this short practice any time, anywhere.

It is very simple. Just silently repeat to yourself, *May you be well* or *May you be happy*, and direct the thought toward someone you know, or toward whomever you encounter. Try spending a day doing this, and observe how you feel at the end of it. This is particularly effective for people you find difficult to deal with, such as a colleague or partner who is upset with you, or a rebellious teenager. Just silently repeat: *May all things go well for you*, and watch how your feelings change. Practicing loving kindness will encourage a more compassionate attitude toward yourself and others.

Walk to become aware of the joy of walking.

Relaxation Comes First

Stress arises when you perceive yourself as being unable to cope. It creates discontent, confusion, and deep tension in you so you do not feel easy with yourself or your body, and consequently suffer from exhaustion, muscular pain, and sleeplessness. Trying to escape from it can cause yet more stress.

If you try to meditate while you are in a stressed or upset state, then it will be much harder to sit peacefully. This is invariably the case if you try to meditate as soon as you get home from work, or to squeeze a meditation period into the middle of a busy day. The moment that you focus on meditating, then all of the tension you are holding in the body and mind becomes more apparent; you become restless or bored, overcome by thoughts or lists of things you must do, or engage in memories of the day's events. If you find you cannot meditate, you might feel there's no hope, and stop trying at all, labeling yourself a failure.

At times like this, it is far more important to relax before you try to meditate. Inner Conscious Relaxation is a technique that has been used for thousands of years to encourage a release of tension on inner levels. You can put your feet up, have a beer or watch a movie, and feel better for a while, but if your inner stress is not dealt with, its physiological effects will continue to drain your energy. It is essential to relax on unconscious levels so the stress response in the body is transformed into a relaxation response. Then, when you begin to meditate, you are clear and receptive mentally.

The Vishuddi chakra symbolizes purification and healing.

To practice Inner Conscious Relaxation, follow the exercise on the next page. You may want to record these instructions on a cassette tape, or write to the authors of this book for a list of their relaxation tapes. Or do it with some friends where one of you reads the directions.

At the beginning and end of each relaxation session, there is an affirmation that you repeat three times, the aim being to give your life greater purpose, strength, and inspiration. Create your own simple statement that expresses what you want to achieve or change in your life — something like, *May I become an instrument of unconditional love,* or *I resolve always to speak the truth of my inner being.*

Inner Conscious Relaxation is also known as *pratyahara,* or the withdrawal of the mind, where you internalize and give rest to the whole of your being. The practice starts with rotating your consciousness around the parts of your body. In this way, you are slowly withdrawing your mind from outside stimulation while maintaining awareness and wakefulness. Silently repeat the name of each part of the body to yourself, visualizing it as you do so. This is followed by a series of visualizations intended to move you through deeply embedded sense impressions in order to release creativity and healing on every level.

Let go and be still.
Become aware of
your body.

Inner Conscious Relaxation

*This relaxation exercise should be
practiced for 20–30 minutes.*

◎ Lie down on the floor with a blanket to cover you and a pillow under
your head so you are comfortable. Take a deep breath and release any
tension. Silently repeat, "I am aware I am practicing Inner Conscious
Relaxation." Watch the *in* and *out* breath for a few moments.

◎ Now create your resolve – i.e., an affirmation concerning your life
that is meaningful to you. Repeat this three times.

◎ Then become aware of your physical body and its point of contact
with the ground ... stay with this awareness for a few moments.

◎ Now rotate your consciousness through your physical body. As
each part of the body is mentioned, silently repeat it and try to
visualize that part in your mind. Go slowly. Right-hand thumb ...
index finger ... second finger ... third finger ... fourth finger ...
palm ... wrist ... lower arm ... elbow ... upper arm ... shoulder ...
armpit ... waist ... hip ... thigh ... knee ... calf ... ankle ... heel ...
sole ... ball of the right foot ... the big toe ... second toe ... third
... fourth ... fifth toe ... left-hand thumb ...index finger ... second
finger ... third finger ... fourth finger ... palm ... wrist ... lower arm
... elbow ... upper arm ... shoulder ... armpit ... waist ... hip ...

... calf ... ankle ... heel ... sole ... ball of the left foot ... the big toe ... second toe ... third ... fourth ... fifth toe ... left shoulder blade ... right shoulder blade ... spinal cord ... the whole of the back ... right buttock ... left buttock ... genitals ... pelvis ... stomach ... navel ... left chest ... right chest ... center of the chest ... neck ... chin ... jaw ... upper lip ... lower lip ... both lips together ... tongue ... nose tip ... right cheek ... left cheek ... left temple ... right temple ... right ear ... left ear ... left eye ... right eye ... right eyelid ... left eyelid ... left eyebrow ... right eyebrow ... center of the eyebrows ... forehead ... top of the head ... back of the head ... whole body, awareness of the whole body.
Notice your breathing for a few moments.

◉ Now focus on the area around your heart. Breathe in, to the heart space in your chest. Now visualize a red rose, a beautiful many-petaled red rose, in your heart. Visualize it slowly opening with each breath you take ... smell its sweet scent ... feel the soft texture of the petals ... drink in the red color ... as the flower opens, your heart opens like a beautiful flower.

◉ Remember the resolve you made at the beginning of this practice. Repeat it three times to yourself.

◉ Just watch your breathing for a few minutes, then move your fingers and toes. Externalize your consciousness. When you are ready, slowly roll over onto your side, then gently sit up.

Identify and release areas of tension to achieve deep relaxation.

Breath of Life

O *ur breath is our best friend. You cannot own it, yet it is with*
you all the time. It is yours to take in and use, or to give
away. The rhythm of your breathing responds to every emotional
state you experience. "Hot" emotions like anger make breathing
shallow and fast; stress and panic make you take short breaths
from the upper chest; while sadness causes great gulping irregular
ones. While you are deeply relaxed, you take deeper, longer breaths.

As breathing so reflects our emotional states, you can use it to induce
relaxation by making a conscious effort to breathe more deeply. When
you feel tense, short, shallow breaths only serve to prolong and sometimes even intensify that feeling. When you bring your breathing down,
your stress levels are immediately reduced. Try this exercise for yourself and discover how learning to regulate your breathing can help to
enhance the quality of your life:

Focus on the breath
of life and be aware
of your feelings.

◉ Close your eyes and start to breathe only with the upper
chest. This makes your breathing very short and shallow.
Observe the emotions that arise in you as you do this.

◉ Now try breathing into your chest at the level of your
lungs. This is how most of us breathe if we are not
distressed or upset. Note how this makes you feel.

○ Now see if you can breathe all the way down into your abdomen —
focus your attention about an inch below your belly button. This
will mean taking much longer, deeper breaths. Notice how breathing
this way makes you feel. If you find this difficult, then try doing it
lying down, which will allow your diaphragm to relax and your lungs
to open more fully. You may wish to repeat *soft belly* as you do this.

Did you notice how much more relaxed you were when you
breathed into your abdomen rather than your upper chest? Remember
to do this every time you begin to panic or feel tense. Just stop for a
few minutes and breathe deeply. Changing your breathing patterns and
becoming conscious of your breath will move you into an aware and
quiet space very quickly.

Breathing techniques can also be used for handling physical pain.
Instead of resisting pain, allow yourself to relax into it, using your
breath to soften yourself toward it and deepen your acceptance of it.
Silently repeat *soft belly*. In the same way, you can use the breath when
your emotions are painful or hot — just take a moment to soften and
breathe. If you are worried about something — soften and breathe.
When it all seems too much to bear — soften and breathe.

Breathing is used throughout all of the traditions of meditation
because it is so rhythmic. By watching the breath, you easily become
focused in the present moment. As you think about the breath coming
into the body, your attention is drawn inward, and you become more
in tune with what is happening inside of you rather than constantly
being pulled into external events. Through watching your breathing,
you begin to calm the mind and can enjoy the experience of profound
levels of concentration and joy.

Pranayama – Alternate Breathing Practice

PRACTICE PAGE

Alternate breathing stores *prana*, or vital energy, in the body.

This is an ancient yoga practice that helps you to develop concentration, as well as balancing and calming the nervous system. The word pranayama *is a Sanskrit word meaning to control the* prana, *known as the breath, life force, or chi. This practice awakens the life force within us, and is refreshing and rejuvenating. If you are feeling distressed, tired, or agitated, try a few minutes of pranayama and see how much better you feel afterward. If you can, practice for 15–30 minutes.*

● Sit comfortably in an upright chair or cross-legged on the floor – whichever feels most natural to you. Settle your body so you feel completely at ease. Using your right hand, place your thumb on your right nostril, your first two fingers on the space between your eyebrows, and the last two fingers on your left nostril. (If you prefer, you can use the left hand, placing the thumb on the left nostril, and so on, reversing all the instructions given below.) You can use your other hand to support your elbow if you need to. Close your eyes and try to relax.

24

- Lightly close off your right nostril with your thumb, and breathe in through your left nostril. Then close off your left nostril with your last two fingers, open your right nostril and breathe out through the right. Breathe in through your right nostril, then close it off with your thumb, open the left nostril, and breathe out through it. Now open both nostrils and breathe in and out. That is one round. Do a few more rounds until you feel quite comfortable with the practice.

- Continue for another five rounds, this time equalizing the length of each in and out breath. Aim to count to five on each inhalation and exhalation. Then remove your hand and just sit quietly for a few minutes, breathing naturally, before opening your eyes.

Use the fingers to change the flow of breath.

- To go further with this practice, you can lengthen the exhalation. Try to double it in relation to the inhalation. Start with ten counts to five – that is, inhale as you count to five, and exhale as you count to ten. As your breathing relaxes and deepens, you can extend the time. Do not over-breathe – you are not trying to prove how long a breath you can take, nor do you want to hyperventilate, but simply to relax more deeply. It takes practice to master the technique successfully and smoothly, but the results will be rewarding.

Creative Visualization

The power of the mind is vast — just as negative or distressed mind-states can cause problems in the body, and profound mental anguish, so positive ones can bring about healing and calm to your whole being. All psychological states and emotions that you experience affect the physical body as much as the mind, so you always have the choice to change how you are thinking in order to create better health. You can induce positive states through creating specific visualizations that release endorphins and stimulate relaxation, inner peace, acceptance, and forgiveness.

Visualization is a form of meditation that has been used by people throughout the world in order to develop concentration, focus, and one-pointedness, as well as to connect them with deeper states of awareness and to develop certain attributes like mental strength, devotion, and wisdom that lead to the enlightened mind. Shamanic traditions use visualization to create an inner journey where images and visions arise spontaneously from a person's unconscious or the higher consciousness, while the yoga tradition uses visualization to awaken latent states of consciousness and perception.

For relaxation and a positive mental state, create a beautiful, tranquil scene — one that has meaning for you. Visualize yourself walking by the sea or in the countryside, being soothed by the waves or trees, listening to birds singing, and feel the sun warming your body.

Enter into the creative mind of colors and images.

This way, you reduce the effect of the stress response in your body and experience a state of inner calm and peace that allows you to remain at ease after the practice is over. See pp. 28–29 for an example of this kind of Creative Visualization practice.

Another visualization method to use is the following, which develops concentration and devotion. Here you use a single object, such as a candle, a picture, or an icon symbolizing an object of devotion. Sitting quietly, gaze with open eyes at that candle flame, picture, or icon until your mind has steadied and you are becoming more focused. Then close your eyes and try to re-create the image inside your mind. You may need to repeat this a few times to clarify the image, but eventually you will be able to see it. In the case of the icon or the picture, you simply re-create the image until you feel as if you are merging with the beloved or the object of devotion.

Many people believe they cannot visualize, but actually everyone can; we simply may not all do it in the same ways. For instance, we are all able to recognize our own car among many in a parking lot, because we carry a mental image of it in our minds.

In visualization, you are not trying to "see" the image literally, but rather to allow your inner senses to perceive it. You may imagine hearing a bird singing or smell the scent of flowers more easily than you can create mental pictures, but each is a valid way of experiencing the effect of creative visualization. As you progressively relax, so your capacity to visualize will be enhanced.

Visualization Practice

PRACTICE PAGE

Visualization can be done while sitting in a comfortable chair (but not so comfortable that you fall asleep!) or lying on the floor. Practice for 20–30 minutes. Make sure that you have a blanket to cover you, because your body temperature will drop as you lie still. Have a small pillow for your head, if you like. If you are sitting, then have both feet on the floor and your hands in your lap. If you are lying down, then have your legs slightly apart and your hands by your sides, palms facing upward. Close your eyes.

A lighted candle helps to create a tranquil atmosphere.

You can escape the stresses of city life through visualization.

- Take a few deep breaths and exhale by blowing out. Now relax your whole body by becoming aware of your feet, slowly bringing your awareness up your body, scanning for any tension and letting it go ... in your legs ... buttocks ... up your back ... breathing and relaxing ... slowly up the front of your body ... to your chest ... taking an extra deep breath and gradually letting it go until your lungs are empty ... then relaxing your hands ... and up your arms to your shoulders and neck ... letting the tension go ... and finally to the whole of your head. Take a deep breath and let it go.

- Then begin to focus on the *in* and *out* flow of your breath, watching it for a few moments. Feel that with each breath you are sinking into a deeper and more peaceful state, becoming quieter.

◉ Now imagine you are walking through a city. All around you are cars and traffic, and you can hear the noise, smell the fumes ... You turn off the main road and begin to walk down a quieter street, where there are outdoor cafés and people talking together ... Soon you are in a more suburban street where children are playing, houses have front yards, and there are trees.

This street leads you to a gentle river ... There is a small boat waiting for you, and you row yourself across to the other side where you can see green fields stretching ahead of you ... You land and walk up the bank to find yourself in the countryside ... You smell the wildflowers as you walk down a small lane between two green fields ... You hear birds calling and feel warmed by the sun on your back.

You notice a small cluster of trees, and the grass beneath them looks soft and inviting ... You lie down and let yourself sink into this natural world that cradles and holds you ... You feel lulled by the sweet smells and sounds, and the gentle breeze caresses your skin ... Stay in this place for as long as you like, and enjoy absorbing the feeling of contentment it gives you.

When you are ready, slowly sit up. All around you is peace, and you feel that same peace inside you ... You know this is something you can keep and take home with you.

◉ Now gently let the visualization fade and become aware of your physical body. Have a good, gentle stretch and open your eyes. Take a deep breath and let it go.

Visualize yourself crossing a river to reach a beautiful haven on the other side.

Clearing the Mind

One of the main forms of meditation practice focuses on concentration on the breath as a means to develop a clear mind. Through focusing on the flow and rhythm of the in and out breaths, the mind begins to become one-pointed, free of distractions and discursive thinking – simply present, here and now. Obviously this may take some time, especially if you are used to thinking or doing many things at once, but even in your first attempts, you will experience a different quality of being, an awareness of an inner spaciousness and peace.

Free your mind by concentrating on the rhythm of the breath.

Through meditation practice, you begin to see yourself more clearly – there is nothing to distract or entertain you except the contents of your own mind! That may seem a bit awesome, especially if you think that what you will find is not so nice, but it is like looking at a mirror covered in dust. When you first look, all you see is the dust; you cannot see a clear image. As you gradually remove the dust, you begin to see your true reflection with greater clarity.

When you first begin to meditate, the mind can appear overwhelming – as if there is this endless drama going on all the time and you are a somewhat unwilling participant. But meditation does not leave you there. It connects you to a deeper place inside yourself where you can see that all the dramas are just that – dramas – and that they come and go. You notice how the mind oscillates from thought to thought or leaps from desire to desire, unsatisfied by its search for pleasure. You see that the source of your fulfillment lies within yourself, not outside, and learn to work toward achieving this.

Meditation opens you up to new possibilities. For instance, as you observe how the mind is constantly presenting you with desires – with a longing for more, or for things to be different from how they are – you also see that you have the choice to be driven by these desires, or to step back so they no longer dominate or control you. You start to create more open space between the endless dramas in the mind and your participation in them, until their power becomes diminished.

Your experiences in meditation can have a profound effect on the rest of your daily life. Many people express how they notice that if they do not start with at least a few minutes of meditation every morning, their day is more stressful, chaotic, or confusing. This time spent in quiet stillness gives you the clarity to cope with pressurizing situations as they arise, so you do not become lost in internal dramas. Greater creativity is allowed as less distraction occurs in your mind.

Let go of your thoughts and desires, and free your true power.

During meditation, you use the breath as an anchor or home base, the place to which you return when the mind drifts. The more you do this, the more you begin to clear the mind's confusion and habit of thinking endlessly, and begin to experience clarity – moments that are free of thinking, where you are poised in the present moment.

Breath Awareness Meditation

The Manipura chakra at the naval represents the solar plexus, which stores *prana*.

T*his is probably the most important meditation method to practice. It forms the basis of all other meditations, establishing clear, one-pointed awareness. Practice it for 20–30 minutes, or longer if you like.*

Before beginning the practice, first find a comfortable place to sit – such as a straight-backed chair or on the floor (see page 54 for more details on posture).

During the practice, you will be focusing on the *in* and *out* flow of your breath. You can do this by focusing on one of the three places. Choose whichever feels most natural to you: the tip of your nose, watching the point where the breath actually enters; the center of your chest, watching it rise and fall; or the area about an inch below your belly button. If you are feeling particularly agitated or stimulated, it is advisable to focus on the latter; but if you are feeling sleepy or lethargic, try focusing on your nose-tip. Experiment with all three places until you find the one that works best for you.

◉ Establish your posture and take a deep breath. Now begin to focus on the rhythm of your breathing, simply watching its natural movement without trying to change it in any way.

◉ In order to help you to concentrate, you can do one of two things:

1 Silently count at the end of each *out* breath: breathe in, breathe out, *one*; breathe in, breathe out, *two*; continuing to count in this way up to ten, and then starting with *one* again. Do this for at least ten minutes. When you feel established in this rhythm, you can change to counting at the beginning of each *in* breath, i.e., *one*, breathe in, breathe out; *two*, breathe in, breathe out, and so on, up to ten as before. Changing your focus from the end to the beginning of the breath deepens your concentration. After a further ten minutes, if you feel your mind is quiet enough, you can drop the counting and just silently watch your breath.

2 Alternatively, you can silently repeat *in, out,* with each *in* and *out* breath. If this is not enough to focus your mind, then repeat *breathing in, breathing out,* or *breathing in peace, breathing out peace,* with each breath, and continue this until the end of the practice.

◉ As you watch the breath, also be aware of other sensations, such as your body's movements, temperature, aches, or discomforts. Try to observe this without judgment. If you have many thoughts, simply label them as thinking or distraction and let them go.

Breath Awareness Meditation is very simple – all you are doing is being aware of your breath. The counting or phases are just to help you keep focused. Use them until you feel as if your mind is quiet.

Entering into the flow of the breath calms and focuses the mind.

Insight to Inner Self

The Ajna chakra, between the eyebrows, is the third eye of inner wisdom.

As you remove the dust on the mirror and see yourself more clearly, you find that you are not hopeless, stupid, or inept as you may have thought, but that actually you have resources of inner strength, self-assurance, and wisdom that you can draw upon constantly. Within each of us is far greater potential and strength than we normally realize; meditation enables us to tap into these resources. Experiencing the quiet within you gives you an added dimension — a still center — from which to relate to yourself and your world. You become less blown about by events and other people, and more stable in your own understanding or perspective.

How often do you really trust your own thoughts, views, or insights? Are you likely to override your own opinions with those of someone else, and to believe that another person's, or even public, opinion carries more weight than your own?

We live in a society that is dominated by group views – a slim body is beautiful while a fat one is not, having lots of money will make you happy – so it is not always easy to go against the grain and discover what is good or true for ourselves, especially if it is different from what is mainstream. We are not taught how to think independently and to trust our own views, nor how to listen to the voice inside us rather than the public one outside.

Meditation connects you to your own insight. Simply by observing whatever arises in the mind, you begin to touch a deeper place where innate wisdom resides. Trusting that wisdom gives you a tremendous sense of relief as you begin to respond to your true self – as if you are being honest with yourself for the first time.

Insight is not the same as intuition – it is not a vague possibility, but a direct, clear knowing; just as you know that the sky is blue, there is no doubt, no questioning. The insights you gain in meditation arise from simply seeing what is, without preconceptions, judgment, or doubt.

As you practice Insight Meditation (see pages 36–7), you become aware of thoughts coming and going, and of physical and emotional sensations. You simply sit and watch. Slowly, it becomes clear how everything arises and dissolves, but nothing remains the same or is permanent. This awareness that all things are impermanent applies to everything. There is nothing that is fixed, solid, or permanent; nothing lasts forever. All things move in a flow of coming and going, including ourselves, our feelings, worries, fears, and difficulties. This realization is tremendously liberating. It is an insight into the essential nature of all things, which leads to great freedom and joy.

Accept that everything in life is impermanent, by nature.

Insight Meditation

PRACTICE PAGE

This meditation teaches focused, one-pointed awareness, so that the pull of ordinary existence does not distract you. Abiding naturally, you are at ease, letting the mind be as it is, without judgment or discrimination. The waves of thought subside, the mind rests, and natural wisdom or insight arises. It should be practiced for 20–30 minutes.

◉ Find a comfortable place to sit. Settle your body and take a few deep breaths. Begin to focus on your breath, paying attention to the tip of your nose, chest, or just below your belly button – whichever feels most natural for you. If you start to feel sleepy, focus on your nose-tip; if you feel restless or anxious, then move your attention to the area around your navel.

Be aware of bodily sensations, but do not judge them.

◉ The objective is simply to pay attention, to be fully present in each moment. Start by noticing all the details of your breath – the sensations you experience as air enters and fills your body and then leaves. Notice how the breaths you take may change from sometimes being long to short, deep or shallow, heavy or soft, and how you sometimes take pauses between breaths – all the time breathing naturally and easily. As you breathe, you can silently repeat *in* and *out* with each breath. You are not trying to do or achieve anything – simply be aware of your presence.

● Remain aware of your body and emotions. Note any physical movements that occur and any feelings that arise in you. Label your sensations, so you know them: such as being hot, cold, stiff, relaxed, tight, warm, soft, or feelings like sad, happy, angry, peaceful, etc. As you observe, notice what happens. Then come back to moment-by-moment awareness of the breath.

● As thoughts or feelings arise, stay aware of them. Mentally note *thinking* or *feeling* and return to being aware of your breath. Sometimes you will only become conscious that you have been thinking after you have been doing it for a while. When you find you are wandering, note *wandering*. Do not judge your thoughts or the activity itself, or condemn yourself – simply be aware of what is happening. Notice mental and emotional sensations and label them appropriately: fear, anxiety, doubt, irritation, restlessness, boredom, depression, joy, etc. If you become distracted, simply note *distraction*; if you are disturbed by sounds, note *hearing* or *disturbance*.

After your meditation, slowly stretch to wake the physical body

● Watch the coming and going of each sensation, thought, or feeling, and of each breath. Remain receptive and in the present. As you observe each moment made, the truth of that moment will become clear.

When you are ready, take a deep breath and let it go. Open your eyes and, very gently, begin to stretch your body.

Making Friends with Yourself and Your World

If you accept yourself, you hold the world in the palms of your hands.

The Buddha experienced spiritual enlightenment through meditation.

*M*editation is an exciting adventure into yourself.
It does not just focus on developing concentration,
but also on opening the heart and developing acceptance,
loving kindness, compassion, and joy. These qualities help you to
free the mind from engaging in any self-negating tendencies it may
have. Many of us spend much of our lives being uneasy with,
if not actually disliking, ourselves. It is essential, if you are to
progress on the path of enlightenment, to accept yourself
just as you are.

The Loving Kindness practice (see pages 40–41) starts with developing loving kindness toward yourself before going on to developing it toward others. This meditation was first taught by the Buddha over two thousand years ago and is a well-tried method for opening the heart.

The Buddha recognized the need for us to make friends with ourselves, to stop rejecting, punishing, or disliking ourselves, or feeling guilty and shameful, and to transform those feelings into ones of forgiveness, acceptance, and love. He saw that we cannot really love anyone else – truly and unconditionally – if we have not first made peace inside by learning to love ourselves. Then we are able to extend that love toward all beings, whoever they may be.

This form of meditation enables you to see how easily you judge and make yourself wrong, and how little you believe that you deserve to be happy or loved. If you do not see yourself as being lovable, how can anyone else? Here you give yourself "space" to drop your resistance and self-dislike and to simply reside in the heart, embracing yourself just as you are, holding yourself as a mother would hold her child, with tenderness and warmth. Soon we go beyond being limited by how we feel about our looks, or our silly behavior, or our embarrassments, and discover that we are very worthy of being cared for and loved, so we become our own best friend.

The meditation then leads you through different stages, as you slowly extend the love you have found in your heart toward those who are nearest and dearest: your family, friends, and those who have helped you in your life; then to those who you do not even know — strangers who, like us, walk this earth and breathe the same air; and finally toward all beings everywhere, releasing your prejudices and fears so that you can love unconditionally.

Children instinctively show us how to care and love.

In this way, you bring awareness and kindness to our world. You eventually appreciate that you are not alone here, and that each of us is worthy of being accepted and loved. We all want to be happy, to be free, and to live peacefully in our world together. By loving yourself, you become a stronger force of love for others, by extending your love into the world, you contribute to greater peace for everyone.

Loving Kindness Meditation

PRACTICE PAGE

*I*n this meditation, you develop metta, *which means to cultivate loving kindness and friendliness. You move through different stages, developing metta toward yourself and others, until your own experience of it grows. The more love you can give, the more will fill your being, for unconditional love is unlimited.*

You should do this practice for 20–30 minutes, staying with each stage for 5–10 minutes.

- Find a comfortable position in which to sit – in a chair or on a cushion on the floor (see page 54). Close your eyes, take a deep breath, and let it go, then let your body settle and relax.

- Start by focusing on your breath while bringing your attention to your heart – or the center of your chest. Then repeat your name, or visualize yourself in your heart just as you are now, so you feel your presence there. Hold yourself there as a mother would her child – gently and tenderly. Silently repeat to yourself, *May I be well, may I be happy, may all things go well for me.* Keep repeating these words in your heart.

    As you do this, release any tension on your *out* breath and breathe in loving kindness. Be aware of any resistance – any reasons you have for why you are not worthy of being happy, or why you should not love

Express thanks to spiritual teachers who have given you inspiration.

yourself. Acknowledge these feelings and then let them go. Continue repeating, *May I be well, may I be happy, may all things go well for me.*

The Buddha is said to have stopped a charging elephant by radiating kindness to it.

◉ Now focus on people who are important to you – your family and friends. Bring them into your heart one by one, visualizing them or repeating their name. Silently repeat, *May you be well, may you be happy, may all things go well for you.* Let go of any past conflicts regarding them as you breathe out, and breathe in happiness and joy. (If you find it easier, you can focus on just one person each time you practice.)

◉ Now think of someone you do not know and have no feelings for – perhaps someone you saw on a train or in a store. Feel friendly toward this person as you repeat, *May you be well, may you be happy, may all things go well for you.* As you do this, you will begin to realize that it is not an individual personality that you are loving, but the very essence of being human, and this you share. You walk the same earth. You breathe the same air.

◉ Now imagine your love extending outward toward all beings, in all directions. Open your heart to all beings, whoever they may be, silently repeating *May all beings be well, may all beings be happy, may all things go well for all beings.* Release any prejudice or resistance within you upon the *out* breath and breathe in unconditional acceptance. All beings are worthy of being loved, whoever they are.

◉ Take a deep breath and gently open your eyes again, letting the love you feel in your heart bring a smile to your lips.

Focus on loving kindness toward all other beings.

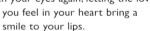

4 1

Opening the Heart
to Forgiveness

When you are in a quiet, meditative state and your heart is open, you not only see more clearly, but are also able to resolve and let go of past difficulties and sadnesses. It is as if the meditation holds you in a healing space, allowing you to expand in awareness.

We all share the same life energy – each one of us is worthy of love.

The Anahata chakra, or heart center, generates love.

Forgiveness is essential if you are to be happy, free, and able to love yourself and others. A lack of forgiveness keeps you locked in a state of inner turmoil, anguish, hate, blame, guilt, or shame. These emotions limit your ability to love and trust. They stop you from being truly joyful – they are like monsters in the dark corners of your mind. Forgiveness is essentially a gift to yourself, for it releases these monsters, allowing you to dance and be free.

Forgiveness is not about just forgetting or putting aside your feelings. It is vitally important that you acknowledge and accept whatever hurt, anger, or shame is present in you, recognizing the depth of your feelings. In order to become a whole, loving, and joyful person, you must reach a state where you heal, forgive, and release the pain.

You are not being asked to forgive atrocities, injustices, or violations, but, rather, the people who committed them. You are forgiving the ignorance and closed-heartedness that blinded them to the level of pain they were inflicting. A person who causes pain is usually feeling great pain in himself. That pain colors his behavior and makes him want to lash out. This also applies to forgiving yourself – you forgive the part of yourself that was blind, uncaring, and filled with pain in the moment when you acted.

It can be very hard to forgive yourself, but it helps to realize that who you were when you did the awful thing is not who you are now. At that time, you were filled with inner conflict and confusion; now you want to be free to love and receive love again. Through meditating, you begin to see who you were, and the emotions that were pouring through you then, but you also experience a kind of spaciousness between who you were and who you are now. This allows you to bring love to your inner pain, which is deeply healing.

In the same way, you can forgive others – forgive them for being in turmoil and for not being able to stop themselves from causing more pain. It does not make them right. It simply releases the intensity of your anguish. Forgiveness comes when you want to heal the pain and put behind you the injustice or shame that caused it, and when you let go of your desire to change others.

You can use the meditation on the next page to bring healing to yourself and to those whom you have wronged, as well as to those who have wronged you. Proceed gently and always hold yourself with love.

Radiate energy from your heart chakra as you open yourself to love.

Forgiveness Meditation

PRACTICE PAGE

In this Forgiveness Meditation, you begin by developing forgiveness for yourself, embracing yourself with love and acceptance. Then you develop forgiveness for someone else, before asking for forgiveness from those whom you have have harmed. The person or persons involved do not have to know — the forgiveness takes place within yourself. You should do this practice for 20–30 minutes, spending 7–10 minutes on each of its stages.

Focus your mind on forgiveness by becoming aware of your heart.

⊚ Find a comfortable position, and sit in a chair or on the floor (see page 54). Make sure your body is at ease, yet alert and upright. Spend a few minutes being aware of your breathing as air enters and leaves your body. Slowly bring your attention to your chest area and heart. With each *in* breath, imagine opening and softening your heart, with each *out* breath, release any tension or stress.

⊚ Now repeat your name or create an image of yourself in your heart. Visualize that image and hold yourself there with care and gentleness. Slowly begin to feel open to forgiving yourself; every moment you practice helps. Silently and slowly repeat, *I forgive myself. I forgive myself. For any harm or pain I may have caused, whether through my words or my actions, I forgive myself.*

Your mind may confront you with all of the reasons why you are not worthy of being forgiven, or with any shame or guilt associated with what you have done. Acknowledge these and then let go of the memories and any resistance in you to them. Keep coming back to the words, to inviting forgiveness. Breathe out any resistance, and breathe in forgiveness. Feel the forgiveness throughout your whole being.

● Now imagine in your heart someone you would like to forgive. Hold them there with your love. Breathe out any resistance, anger, or fear, and breathe in forgiveness. Silently repeat, *I forgive you. I forgive you. For the harm and pain that you have caused, through your words and your actions, I forgive you.*

Remember to have a soft belly, and let your breath relax you. Take your time. Let go of all the reasons why this person should not be forgiven, and remember you are not forgiving what they did, but the ignorance that caused them to act in this way.

Visualize each person as you send or accept forgiveness.

● Now visualize in your heart someone whom you may have hurt or upset. Hold him there with forgiveness and love. Silently repeat, *I ask for your forgiveness. I ask for your forgiveness. For the hurt or pain I may have caused you, through my words or my actions, please forgive me.*

Keep breathing. Accept your own confusion and closed-heartedness. We all make mistakes. It is not who you are now. Feel your heart opening to forgiveness; you do not have to continue suffering. Repeat: *I am forgiven, I am forgiven.* Feel the joy of forgiveness throughout your whole being. You are forgiven. You have forgiven. You have been forgiven.

When you are ready, take a deep breath and slowly let it go. Have a good stretch. Let the joy in your heart greet your world.

Prayer and Devotion

A prayer may be as simple as requesting help or guidance, but, throughout history, it has also been used to open people's hearts to that which is beyond us — to make contact with the divine. This is a powerful form of meditation, for, in deep prayer, you go beyond your sense of self to communicate and merge with a love and wisdom greater than yourself.

Candles, precious books, incense, and sacred objects all aid our practice.

Through prayer, devotion, and ritual, you are absorbed into the love of the divine, or the awakened; you surrender the ego and allow the will of the highest to move through you. Whatever you personally believe represents divinity fills you with inspiration and promotes personal transformation and healing. You can express devotion in as many diverse ways as the divine manifests.

Every religion has its own symbols and expressions. The Sufis are known for the ecstatic dancing of their Whirling Dervishes. Christians sing devotional songs or repeat *Mother Mary*, awakening the power of her love. Buddhists prostrate to an image of the Awakened One as representing the ideal they wish to attain, while Hindus express their devotion in many ways, including chanting mantras (like those of the Hare Krishnas) which invoke the love of Lord Krishna.

Devotion may be shown through celebrating events like harvest festivals or solstices and equinoxes, or anywhere people gather together to sing, pray, celebrate, and express gratitude as a community, sharing our

friendship and support for each other. In this way, the divine is brought into our daily lives. Devotion and respect for the sacred is also expressed in the simple ritual of preparing a meditation place or lighting a candle before you begin to practice.

You can create your own rituals for celebration, or for marking the passing of important moments, in recognition of the divine. In rituals, you can chant mantras, give and receive blessings, make offerings, pray and sing with others, light candles, decorate with flowers, burn incense, read poems or tell stories, and have quiet time together.

Prayer and ritual cultivate a relationship with what is sacred and evokes humility, surrender of the ego and sincerity in practice. You can create your own prayers to reflect your sentiments, and to remind you of love, kindness, generosity, and the magnificence of the human spirit. In this way, you remain connected to the divine, creating a spiritual lifeline. Prayer influences the way you live in the world, encouraging greater tolerance and compassion. Your prayers may be simple and devotional, such as:

- *May your loving presence guide me in my thoughts and actions.*
- *May I be an instrument of your compassion and wisdom.*
- *May I be filled with loving kindness.*
- *May all beings be free from suffering.*

Create a meditative environment with your own precious objects.

Creating a Meditative Environment

It is very helpful to have a special place to go for meditation practice – somewhere simple and quiet – with the idea that, in this place, you come to clear your mind and open your heart. Establishing such a space is an expression of your commitment to your wellbeing.

If you cannot meditate outside, bring nature inside with the sweet smell and colors of flowers.

You see the importance of this when you enter a church or temple, for there the accumulated prayers and meditations of many people have created a sense of the sacred that is almost tangible. After a while, the area where you practice will take on the same atmosphere of the sacred. It will become a place where you immediately feel spacious, replenished, and reconnected with yourself.

Obviously, it is not always possible to have a separate room to use purely for meditation, but it can be just a corner of one, perhaps your bedroom. You could even convert a closet under the stairs if there is no other place – anywhere that you can clear of clutter and make into a quiet space. The area should be symbolic of the clarity you wish to find through meditation. Your environment represents your mind, so a cluttered or messy place symbolizes the part of the mind you are trying to put in order by meditating.

All that you need is a small table for flowers; a candle; any objects or pictures that for you represent the sacred or divine; a chair, stool, or cushion; and a mat on the floor. Face a wall or in a direction that allows you to focus your attention, because facing into the middle of a room can be distracting. You also may want to keep a shawl or light blanket there which you can use to keep warm, and a thicker blanket to lie on for deep relaxation. Some people also wear special loose clothing which they only use for meditation.

Before you sit, make sure your telephone is off and that any other people who are around know that you are meditating. A sign on the door may be enough. It might take them a while to accept what you are doing, but they soon will when they see the positive changes in you.

It is also lovely to meditate outdoors in nature, surrounded by running water, beautiful trees and flowers, with sweet smells in the air. This can put you immediately into a quiet, reflective mood, in which you easily merge with the environment around you. Meditating in a noisy or busy place can be a bit more challenging, and you are less likely to want to merge with such surroundings! However, it is possible to meditate in any busy place, even on a train or bus, by focusing either on your breathing or by extending loving kindness to everyone and everything around you.

Natural surroundings will help you discover your inner strength.

How and When to Practice

*T*he most important contribution you can make to developing
your meditation practice is to practice daily, even if it is only
for a few minutes. These few minutes every day are better than an
hour once a week, as daily practice makes you more conscious of
the meditative mind. Even if five minutes is all you have time for,
you will soon feel the effect of meditation in your daily life if you
do it regularly. Later, you may extend the time to 10, 20, or 30
minutes. It is better to want to practice, rather than to feel
that you ought to. If you do too much too soon, you may feel
uncomfortable and not do it again for a while. So start with brief
periods. Let the time you practice extend itself naturally.

On the other hand, it is very easy to do only a few minutes' practice a
day and to not really give yourself the chance to experience going
beyond the busyness of your mind to the quiet within. Feelings of
doubt, frustration, and boredom often arise, and you will have to discipline yourself to continue practicing at such times, rather than
finishing sessions too soon. A good time span to aim for is 20–30 minutes a day, and then to sit for longer when you feel that you can.
Sometimes your body will need a stretch, so then you can do Walking
Meditation, as described on page 86.

Some people like to use an alarm clock so they know when to end their meditation session. This means that you do not have to stop to check the time but can really surrender to the practice. However, do use a gentle, quiet alarm so that you are not unduly disturbed by a loud noise!

The early morning is always recommended as the best time of day to practice, since this is when you are feeling most alert, not yet having experienced the pressures of the day. It is usually a quiet time, before the world begins to belong to humans again. However, for some people mornings are very busy and filled with family demands, so adding something else to do may seem impossible. Whatever happens, do not make the idea of meditating into another form of stress. Perhaps you should rise earlier, or simply find a different time in the day that works better for you.

Late evening is often a good time to meditate, when the world is becoming quiet again after the hectic activity of the day – perhaps before you go to bed, if you are not feeling too tired. Try not to meditate just after you have eaten, as your full stomach will make it hard for you to focus successfully on your breathing and you will probably become sleepy.

Once you have found a good time to practice, there will always be other things to divert you and attempt to claim your attention. However, committing yourself to meditating at a certain time every day means making a commitment to your own sanity and wellbeing. Make it a priority, and something you really want to do. It is important for everyone to find time for themselves and the things they enjoy doing, and once you have decided you wish to make meditation part of your daily life, you will soon see the benefits.

Clarifying Priorities

The Muladhara chakra at the base of the spine symbolizes spiritual potential.

Making time to meditate is not just about moving your schedule around. It is also about making a commitment to yourself — to your peace, to having a clear mind and an open heart, to making friends with yourself and your world. No one else can do this for you. You must have reached the point where your wellbeing has become your priority.

Many people say that they would love to meditate, but they just don't have time. However, when you don't take time to be with yourself, and instead are busy all the time — caring for others, working, or being entertained — you put yourself in danger of burning out. After a while, inevitably, you start to grow irritable, annoyed, resentful, tired, short-tempered, or overwhelmed. You may be unable to sleep, or begin to feel unappreciated or unloved. You forget about joy and laughter. When that happens, your resentment and irritation influence your behavior, and you have a detrimental effect on those around you.

It can seem selfish to want to spend time alone to practice meditation in the midst of a busy life; it can easily make you feel guilty. But taking time for self-reflection is actually a selfless activity, for by finding peace in yourself, the quality of care you give to others becomes more loving. As you make friends with yourself, you find it natural to feel loving toward others. You become more happy and tolerant, so that everyone benefits. Create balance in your life by making time to meditate while continuing to respond to family and work demands.

Making this your priority may require a certain shift in your attitude. You must begin to recognize that your own needs are just as important as those of others. You are a priority. It means making the effort, developing the motivation and persistence to continue your practice, despite any opposition. Rather than putting meditation last on your list of things to be done, put it first. After you meditate, doing the dishes or going to work will seem much more pleasant! The more you practice, the more you will benefit – you will feel alive and joyful rather than weary and bad-tempered.

A little space is all you need to create a meditative environment.

When you make the decision to put your happiness first, it helps to enlist the support of your family. Even if they do not want to practice with you, if you can make them understand that this will not only help you, but will help you care for them, you will find they are often very tolerant. Certainly, they will soon see how much more at peace you are and how stress begins to affect you less and less.

Try making a commitment to meditate regularly for a week, and see how you feel. Then extend this period to a month, and so on. Allow yourself the time to change and it will happen, bringing great benefits to both you and those around you along with it.

Meditation Posture

Sitting in the right posture is essential for meditation. The wrong posture will cause you discomfort, and any pain you feel will distract your mind from focusing on the practice. So take some time to experiment with the different postures suggested here until you find the one that works for you.

The most important aspect of your meditation posture is having a straight back. There are a number of reasons for this. First, sitting upright makes it much easier to breathe. When your back is even slightly bent, your lungs are compressed, making it harder to follow the *in* and *out* flow of the breath.

Second, a straight back has the effect of helping you feel alert, dignified, and awake – all qualities that you want to bring to your meditation. A bent or rounded back is a posture associated with sadness, hopelessness, and depression – not qualities you want to stimulate in meditation!

And third, when the back is upright, it naturally supports itself so the muscles do not start to ache. If you are slightly bent, the muscles have to work really hard to keep you in that position, and soon they will start to ache, causing a distraction for you. So any position that gives you a straight back is correct.

While sitting, it is also important that your shoulders are relaxed. Do not cross your arms; rest your hands in your lap or thighs, so your shoulders are not pulled out of line. Your head should face

Straighten your spine to open the chest and allow the lungs to expand.

forward – neither up nor down. Your eyes may be
feel sleepy, in which case they can be open but lowe
trained on the ground a few feet in front of you.

Here are a few sitting postures to try:

- In a straight-backed chair; sit with your feet placed firmly
  ground; sit upright, rather than leaning back in your chair. A
  the small of your back can help enormously. You may also wa
  put a pillow or folded blanket under your feet (1).
- A kneeling stool, as found in many office-supply and back specia
  stores, enables the spine to be straight without putting any pressure
  on the legs. You may want to set a small pillow on your lap upon
  which to rest your hands (2).
- A meditation stool, along with a pad or folded blanket under your
  buttocks and legs, means there is no pressure on your shin bones.
  Instead of a stool, you can straddle a pile of firm cushions (3).
- One or two (or more) firm cushions for sitting cross-legged can be
  used so the base of your spine is raised higher than your knees,
  which ensures circulation. It also helps to place a pad or folded
  blanket under you to support your ankles. Try sitting with one leg in
  front of the other, or with one ankle on top of the other (4).

A comfortable
posture minimizes
the distraction of
physical discomforts.

| 1 | 2 | 3 | 4 |

Training the Mind

The first thing you will notice when you sit still and meditate is how busy your mind is. It seems as if there is endless babble or dialogue going on, with one drama after another — ranging from making shopping lists to recalling past conversations to deciding what to wear at a meeting next week, etc. The mind seems much noisier than you have ever known it, and it seems impossible to focus on anything.

However, the truth is that the mind is always this busy and distracted; it is simply that you are normally not quiet enough to notice. Your usual state of externalization, where you are pulled in one direction after another, obscures the ongoing dialogue inside you. So when you finally pay attention, the noise can seem deafening.

It may be a reassuring thing to know that we are all like this. You are not alone! Although true meditation occurs in the space between thoughts — in the moments when the mind rests — those moments may be rare and short-lived. Many of us spend our thirty minutes a day *practicing* how to meditate — slowly learning how to become quieter, how to let thoughts go. We discover that the breath or the object of the practice can act as an anchor that brings the mind to a state of calm.

Soar above the noise of your thoughts to a quiet place.

It is normal to be thinking while you are practicing. Someone once estimated that you can have 2,300 thoughts per half hour – all the time while trying not to think! But if you persevere, what you will notice is that your thoughts become quieter and less dominating. There are more spaces, more moments of stillness between them. In those moments, you know throughout your being why you are doing this. It makes you feel as though you have come home.

What is important is that you do not make any judgments about yourself for thinking; do not make yourself wrong or hopeless for being unable to follow instructions, that you will never become quiet, so you may as well give up now. Judging yourself in this way is actually just another distraction. And anyway, if you are going to judge yourself, you may as well judge everyone, for we all do the same. Remember, you are *practicing* meditation; you are not yet a master of it. Just sitting still for half an hour is a miracle in itself, so enjoy the time. You are training your body to be still, and the more you focus on the practice, so your mind will also become trained.

During your meditation, you can release thinking patterns by labeling them as thinking, or by visualizing them as birds in the sky of your mind, and letting them fly away. Try not to judge yourself to harshly – be patient and take your time. Learn to accept yourself, making friends with the act of meditating, and discover how it can set you free too.

Witness Meditation

PRACTICE PAGE

The purpose of this meditation is to develop an objective awareness of yourself so you do not become caught in the dramas created by your mind. It allows you to experience an inner "spaciousness" where you can see clearly. You should practice this for 20–30 minutes if possible.

- Start by finding a comfortable place to sit. Take a deep breath and spend a few moments concentrating on settling your body and your breathing pattern.

Observe the process of body and mind.

- Now become aware of your body. Move your mind through your body, slowly noticing each part, starting with the toes ... feet ... legs ... knees ... thighs ... buttocks ... lower back ... middle back ... and upper back. Be aware of the whole of your back. Then observe your genitals ... pelvis ... abdomen ... chest ... breasts. Take a deep breath and observe how your chest rises and falls with each breath. Then be aware of your fingers ... hands ... arms ... elbows ... shoulders ... neck ... jaw ... mouth ... nose ... eyes ...ears ... forehead ... and the back of your head ... your whole body.

Now become aware of your breathing ... observe the air as it comes into your body ... how your body moves as it breathes ... and the way the air leaves. Be aware of the pauses between breaths. Notice the temperature and quality of your breath. Watch this for a few minutes.

Now become aware of your thinking ... let your thoughts arise spontaneously, without judgment ... good or bad is unimportant, just observe ... see how your thoughts come and go ... notice how one thought leads to another ... be a witness to the processes of your mind. Note what happens as you pay attention to your thoughts.

Experience the noise surrounding you and the contrasting quiet of the mind.

Now send your awareness out ... into the room you are sitting in ... then into the street ... farther and farther ... until you can "see" a mile away all around you. Externalize your awareness. Be aware of all the sounds around you, but do not focus on any particular one ... just notice the sounds of life ... become aware of the world around you. Observe this for a few minutes.

Now bring your awareness back to the breath flowing in and out of your nostrils ... become conscious of your physical body and its contact with the seat or floor beneath you ... take a deep breath and let it go. Give yourself a gentle stretch.

Overcoming Obstacles

It would be wonderful if, on coming to sit for meditation with mindful awareness, you immediately entered into a state of bliss and stayed there for the whole session. However, the likely scenario is that you will confront issues like boredom, lethargy, restlessness, anxiety, doubt, desire, dislike — and so on. The mind is not used to being still and will find numerous ways to create distractions. Luckily, there are some remedies you can apply, for instance:

- A first-aid remedy that cures many different ailments is *effort*. You have to apply effort in order to stay focused on practicing, and prevent you from drifting. Effort keeps you focused. You can remind yourself why you are here, what your intention is (i.e., to meditate), that it will not be for very long, and that all you have to do is stay aware for these few minutes.

- For dullness or sleepiness, try meditating with your focus on the tip of your nose; have your eyes open but gazing (unfocused) at the ground in front of you; or stand up and walk mindfully around the room and get a breath of air before coming back to your seat.

- For restlessness, try practicing Inner Conscious Relaxation to release tension before you begin to meditate, or meditate with your focus in your abdomen; this will quieten your energy.

● For anxiety, try to focus more closely on the rhythm of your breath. Bring your awareness of your breath to your abdomen, rather than to your chest, where it may reside if you are anxious. Those short, shallow breaths won't calm you, but you'll find the rhythm of longer, deeper breaths from your abdomen much more soothing.

● You may doubt what you are doing and wonder what the purpose of all this is. Doubt is very useful, since it makes us question and go deeper. Keep questioning. Have you noticed any changes? Do you feel any benefits from meditating? Don't practice because you think you ought to; do it because you feel better for it.

● Desire can range from the longing for things to be different to a great yearning for a frosted cake. By paying attention and recognizing desire as simply desire, you can learn to be with what is. You can develop a deep appreciation for things as they are, recognizing the beauty and abundance that surrounds you.

● Among the many emotions that may arise is aversion or dislike of yourself or someone else. Without getting carried away by the emotion, you can cultivate kindness, particularly by practicing the Loving Kindness meditation.

● Awareness enables you to observe what is happening in your mind – its thoughts, images, and memories – and how you are feeling emotionally. If you practice nonjudgment, and have genuine self-acceptance and patience, then your mind will slowly become quieter and your experience of peace will deepen.

Mantra Meditation

PRACTICE PAGE

A mantra is a meaningful sound or phrase that, when repeated either silently or out loud, calms and stills the mind, releasing it from its habitual thinking patterns. The mind becomes totally absorbed and anchored in the sound and, by repeating the mantra, lets go of its need for external entertainment. Mantra repetition is like a broom that sweeps your mind free of trash. It focuses the mind, allowing it to enter deeper into consciousness.

A string of beads can be used to count your mantra during meditation.

The use of mantras is common to all religions and spiritual traditions, involving the repetition of the name of a sacred being, such as Mary Mother, Jesus, Hare Krishna, or Namo Buddha. Alternatively, many traditions use a word or phrase that has special meaning, such as *Hallelujah, Om* (the sound of the universe), *Om Shanthi* (peace), *Om Mani Padme Hum* (the jewel in the heart of the awakened mind), or *Om Namah Shivaya* (homage to Shiva who transforms negativity). You may use any sound or short phrase that has meaning for you. The repetition may be done silently or aloud, in a formal meditation session, or at any time, anywhere. It can be useful to do it silently at times when other people are present and you need to stay grounded and balanced in yourself.

- ⊚ To practice formally, find a comfortable place to sit with a straight back. Take a few deep breaths and relax. Repeat your mantra, either silently or out loud, use the same mantra throughout your practice.

● The mantra is repeated with full attention on the sound or on the rhythm of the breath. When using a short mantra, repeat it in time to the inhalation and exhalation; for a longer mantra, simply remain aware of the breath while repeating the words. The mantra is an anchor that helps the mind to quieten and become focused. If you find yourself getting distracted or drifting off into discursive thinking, just bring your mind back to your mantra and continue repeating it. Mantra meditation is like spiritual food; it calms the mind, awakens the creative process, nourishes the soul, and opens the heart, bringing joy and happiness.

● You can also use a rosary or *mala* – a string of beads – as a way of focusing. With each repetition of the mantra, you move to the next bead on the string. If you know how long it takes to do one round of the mala, then you can do as many rounds as you wish for your meditation session and you will not need to time yourself with a clock.

Be aware of your breathing as you recite your mantra.

Healing Inner Wounds

As you may remember, the words meditation and medicine come from the same Latin root, so it is not surprising that meditation is often spoken of as a form of healing, especially since it releases the body from the symptoms of stress.

However, in order to be healed, we need to become whole within ourselves (healing and wholeness also have the same root meaning), which is more than just being stress-free. Meditation acts as a healer for psychological, emotional, and physical problems as you develop deeper personal awareness and a greater acceptance of yourself.

With mindful attention, you will learn to recognize and let go of your resistance to certain things and to see the many ways that you ignore your own worries or sidestep emotionally charged situations; in other words, you will begin to accept yourself as you are, in a genuinely honest way. The more that you open your heart to loving yourself, the more you will be able to bring love to those unloved parts of your being — those places you ignore, deny, or repress, the hidden voices and feelings and lost dreams. This is what is meant by making yourself "whole."

You can use the breath in meditation to bring healing — breathing into those places that hurt and letting the pain go with the *out* breath. Then you can breathe into the space that has been left behind once the pain is released.

Very often, we hold onto old hurts, memories, guilt, and anger, for, through such feelings, we have found our identity, thinking: I was an

Let go of your past and experience inner peace.

abused child, I am the son of an alcoholic, my husband left me, I am a terrible person, and so on. The pain gives you an excuse for not really living – how can you trust or love again when you have been so deeply hurt? How can anyone love you when you have behaved so badly? The past provides you with reasons for being as you are now, so how can you let it go, how is it possible for such wounds to be healed? Who would you be without the pain, without the story that makes you what you are?

Healing means having the courage to forgive and let go of the story. Then you yourself as you are in the present, without the baggage of the past. You cannot avoid hurt, loss, suffering, grief, or death; they are part of being alive. But you do not need to hold onto the pain and make it a story that becomes the focus of your life.

In meditation, you learn to breathe and let go, to breathe and forgive, to breathe and come back to yourself as you are in this moment. You discover that you can be with what is hap- pening without being swallowed up by any resentment or hurt that you may feel. You can see the pain, know it, taste it, and then release it and find your healing.

Healing Heart Meditation

PRACTICE PAGE

This meditation opens the heart to healing. Practice it for 20–30 minutes. Start by finding a comfortable place to sit and close your eyes. Spend a few moments watching your breath as your body settles down.

◉ Focus your awareness on your whole physical body. Repeat silently three times: *I am aware of the whole of my body.* Then visualize your body as if it were a temple. You live in this temple your whole life … it is in this temple that healing takes place … bringing you closer to yourself … your peace, your love. Know that your body is a blessing, a great gift.

Heart and mind unite in the Healing Heart Meditation.

◉ Now become aware of the incoming and outgoing breath. Feel how your breath is your best friend … get closer and more familiar with this friend … the closer you are to your breath, the greater your feeling of inner peace.

◉ Now focus on your heart and the center of your chest … breathe into this space, into your heart … this is the source of unconditional love that supports and nourishes your whole being … as you breathe into this area, feel that you are being held by that love, as a mother would hold a child … release any tension with the *out* breath.

- Your heart is like a flower opening in the sun ... visualize in your heart a red rose ... see the petals and their color ... smell the fragrance ... watch the rose opening as you breathe into your heart ... softening and releasing. Know that your true nature is pure, loving energy.

- Imagine holding yourself in your heart gently and tenderly ... this love is healing you. Silently repeat to yourself: *May I be well, may I be happy, may I be healed.* Drop any resistance you experience ... any reasons why you should not be well ... any feelings of not being worthy of happiness or health ... keep breathing into your heart ... feeling this love for yourself as if it were a beautiful flower.

The love for yourself blossoms as awareness grows.

- Your love is your healing ... feel the divine love that supports this earth ... the trees ... the flowers ... the animals ... the oceans ... the stars and the sky. Through your heart, you are at one with the universe ... there is no separation between you and what is outside you. As you love yourself, so universal love will nourish and enrich you.

- Silently repeat: *My body is my temple ... my breath is my friend ... my mind is calm and peaceful ... my heart is loving ... I am pure love ... I am being healed by love.* Your life is a gift to be cherished ... treasure yourself always. It is love that heals ... feel the peace and the joy of this love.

When you are ready, take a deep breath, gently stretch your body, and open your eyes again.

Creative Practices:
Writing, Painting, Singing

Meditation and healing touch the more receptive and creative side of our being, the right brain, as opposed to the more assertive and rational left brain. Participating in creative activities enables you to experience deeper layers of feeling within yourself. This supports the healing process, providing a context for release and acceptance. Here are just a few suggestions for you to try.

WRITING

When you write something, even something as mundane as a shopping list, you no longer have to keep thinking about or trying to remember it. When it comes to your feelings and insights, writing provides a way not only of making things clearer to yourself, but also of taking you deeper into what lies beneath your superficial layer of thoughts. It provides a powerful form of communication with your innermost world, helping to bring your more hidden feelings to the surface where they can be embraced and healed.

Writing and painting often express your subconscious thoughts.

Try keeping a journal. Just write down what your thoughts or feelings are, what is most important for you or uppermost in your mind, and, as you write, let the words write themselves. Write about what is going on inside, about your health, your relationships, your fears, your longings. Start each page with a statement to get you going, and then just let yourself write. Begin with something like: The changes taking place in me are … , How I feel about my life is … , I would like to forgive … , or create your own.

ART

Sometimes feelings cannot be expressed in words and you need to find a non-verbal form of expression – one that allows you to release the feelings so you can make sense of them. Art therapy encourages this. Using paint, crayon, clay, or other substances, you can reach into the depths of your emotions and give them a form.

This can be done in a class with a trained art therapist, or in a setting of your own choice, either by yourself or with others. What you produce is irrelevant; all that matters is what it means to you. Paint whatever you want, but do it spontaneously, without thinking, so that the images seem to paint themselves. Paint your anger, your fear, your joy. Let your feelings speak to you in their language.

Painting can give a deep sense of joy.

SINGING

It can be very difficult to express your feelings, especially if you think they might be inappropriate or unacceptable. Instead they can get locked inside you, hindering your ability to feel alive, and inhibiting your self-expression. Singing is a wonderful way to open your voice and heart, and release blocked energy.

Find your voice by singing in the shower, or perhaps the car, sing along to a favorite song, sing your feelings, your anguish, your happiness. Or try chanting a mantra, such as *om* (see page 62). Just take a deep breath and, on the *out* breath, sound a long *oooo*, followed by closing your mouth and humming a long *mmm*. Keep doing this over and over until you feel your heart rejoicing.

Inner Happiness

The concentric circles of mandalas signify universal harmony.

How easily we can forget that the main reason that we choose to meditate is to become happier! You would not be reading this if you did not think that meditation would help you feel better, grow calmer, become a nicer person, discover your true nature, and even, ultimately, gain enlightenment — all of which adds up to your becoming happier. True happiness is a state of inner peace, a deep abiding contentment without the internal clamoring of unfulfilled desire or fear of change, and a dynamic aliveness that remains constant regardless of circumstances.

Through meditation, you learn that all things are impermanent, fleeting, insubstantial. You observe how not even your thoughts are constant. But meditation also shows us how all things are connected, how nothing exists on its own. For instance, these words you are reading are printed on paper; the paper would not exist if it were not for the clouds and the rain, the earth and the trees, the woodsman, the paper maker, and so on. You could say that the paper actually contains all these things in it, for without any one of them, it would not be here.

In the same way, we are each intimately connected to each other, and to all things. We are not isolated units but are interrelated, made up of everyone we have ever known, everything that has ever happened to us, and everything we have ever eaten or done or thought. Your breath is not separate from your body, and yet it is not your breath. Your body is not separate from the food that you eat, and the food is not separate from the earth, the sun, the water, the farmer, or the cooking pot and spoon, and yet, at the same time, it is none of these things.

Without this awareness, you live in an isolated, lonely world – out of touch with the preciousness of life, disconnected from your source. When you realize that we are all connected to each other and inter-dependent, that we contain all of life within us, then you know yourself to

be an integral part of a universal whole. As you sit in meditation, you experience your relationship to life and can extend your field of aware-ness so that you are no longer isolated or separate, but merge with all of existence.

You are not separate from the sun or the trees or the earth.

Happiness spontaneously arises in you when you stop feeling sepa-rate and let yourself merge fully with the present moment. You may experience great bliss or warmth and a feeling that the heart is open-ing with an outpouring of love. This is natural, because you are connecting with the essence of who you really are. You are not born to suffer. You are here to find joy, passion, and happiness. This is your birthright. In discovering your connectedness, you discover a world that is beautiful, precious, and all of ours to share and care for. You see that we are all co-creators of this world, and that we are responsible for ourselves as well as for each other.

Appreciation Meditation

T*his meditation generates deep appreciation and gratitude for yourself and our world. Find a comfortable place to sit and settle your breathing.*

◉ Begin by developing gratitude for the seat beneath you ... thanking it for supporting you ... appreciating the person who made your seat ... and all the elements that were involved in the making of its different components.

◉ Now extend your gratitude to the building you are in, appreciating its protection and safety ... the space it gives so you can meditate ... all the people who worked to make the building ... the materials that were used to make it, and all the elements that go to make up those materials.

◉ Now cultivate gratitude for the ground beneath you ... that supports and sustains you throughout life ... appreciate the earth that maintains and gives life ... appreciate the trees and plants ... the animals and birds ... the oceans and marine life ... each an interdependent part of the whole.

◉ Now bring your appreciation to your body ... feeling gratitude for the way it nourishes and supports you ... how it enables you to feel love, happiness, and joy ... experience the energy moving through your body, the life force …recognize how your body is connected to the food and water you give it and the air you breathe … appreciate the clothes that keep you warm, feeling gratitude for the plants or animals that provided the material … appreciate the connection your physical body has to all the elements of life.

- Now send gratitude to your parents … without them, you would not have this life … appreciate however much they were able to give you, recognizing whatever difficulties they may have had. Now extend that appreciation to your grandparents and ancestors … for they gave you the color of your eyes, the laughter in your voice, their wisdom and knowledge … appreciate that they have returned to the earth … completing cycles of interdependency.

- Now expand your appreciation to include all beings … recognizing how we are all interdependent … how we all walk this earth together … how we breathe the same air … how we all want to be happy … how within each of us, there is a light … and each light reflects all the other lights.

- Now bring your appreciation to your breath … to the flow of the air as it enters and leaves your body. Remember that we do not own this air; it is only ours to share. Take time to appreciate the air and the life it gives you.

- When you are ready, take a deep breath and gently stretch your body. Once you have done this, bring your appreciation with you into your daily life.

Meditation in Daily Life

Meditation brings awareness into everyday tasks by focusing on the present moment.

Meditation is not just something you do when you sit formally, but is a way of living that can be brought into every aspect of your life. It is seen in the way that you pay attention to the present moment, and in the way that you extend loving kindness to others. It is practiced when you wash the dishes or dig the flowerbeds, read to your children or listen to music.

Meditation is about paying attention, so being aware of how you get up in the morning, how you treat your family and colleagues, how you eat, and how you feel about yourself are all ways that you can practice. In whatever you do, you have the opportunity to be fully present, engaged, aware, and absorbed in the moment.

Being physically active is no hindrance to meditation. For some people, being idle is difficult; work helps to keep them feeling energized. In many monasteries and ashrams in the east, participants are asked to do some hours each day of work, whether it be gardening, cleaning, cataloging books, etc. Very often, the work seems unnecessary – for instance, gardening an area that will soon be swept away in the monsoon, or digging a patch of earth only to fill it in again. What is really being taught is the ability to make work itself a meditation; it is to be done wholeheartedly, with complete attention, and, particularly, without attachment to the outcome or fruit of the labor undertaken.

This approach is revolutionary in the west, where we are purposefully taught to focus on our achievements. Such selflessness can seem impractical to us, since obviously people need to have a balance of work and recompense. But the point of this practice is to focus on your attitude. If you are working with a selfish, self-centered frame of mind, you will probably suffer from stress and burn out quite quickly, accomplishing little. If your activity is for the benefit of others, you will feel happier and more at peace.

Bring awareness to how you treat your family and colleagues.

Work is one area where you can bring meditation alive in everyday life. Another is your relationships.

Close, intimate relationships are one of our greatest challenges – we are all so different with our own ways of thinking, our own needs, feelings, histories, and neuroses, that it sometimes seems a miracle we get along at all! Bringing awareness and compassion into your relationships will also bring deeper understanding and tolerance. You will recognize your own feelings, while also being open to hearing and receiving how someone else feels, without feeling threatened.

You cannot necessarily change the circumstances of your life – where you live, who you live with, the health of your family members, your work – but you can change your attitude toward these circumstances. You can focus on what is wrong, difficult, or overwhelming, or you can focus on what is good, loving, and workable. This is meditation in action.

Practicing Mindfulness

When walking,
just walk –
concentrating on
the task in hand
encourages
mindfulness.

M*indfulness is the art of being aware – of our thoughts,
feelings, behavior, of others and their feelings, and of our
environment. Few of us have any real self-awareness, other than
self-consciousness. We operate from such an "I"-centered
place that objective awareness does not come naturally.
Mindfulness is a way of looking and being in the present
with whatever is happening.*

You start to do this during meditation when you simply watch
yourself breathing. There is breathing, and there is the observer.
You can bring that same awareness to every part of your
life. Mindfulness is simply doing one thing at a time.
When you do more than one thing, you cannot pay
attention fully to what you are doing. When
you talk and eat at the same time, for example, you
do not notice your food, nor savor each bite.

⊚ Pay attention to how you move, eat, and behave.
When you walk, be aware of your muscles moving, of
the space in which your body moves. When you eat, be
aware of the taste and texture of your food. When
you wash dishes, pay attention to the water and soap
bubbles. When you brush your teeth, notice the
activity of brushing.

- Notice your thoughts, desires, feelings, watching them come and go, noticing impermanence. Do not judge; just watch and accept what is. Notice your thinking patterns and reactions, your habits and criticisms. Watch how you make excuses, how self-doubt and fear arise, how you label yourself and others. Notice how hard it is to be still, how you fill empty spaces with things to do and people to see. Watch your mind at play and in this way come to know yourself.

- As you grow in awareness of yourself and accept whatever you find, deeper issues may start to arise. In your responses to people or situations, you will begin to see how the past has influenced the way you think and feel. Recognize your history in your present, and know you can heal that history, rubbing balm onto those old wounds. Through mindful attention, you will come to know yourself more deeply, and from this will come peace.

- Pay attention to those around you. Being mindful means being able to respond to needs that are unvoiced, to recognize feelings without having to be told. Listen and receive the other person without having to change or fix them, without judging them, and without comparing them to yourself.

Be aware during daily routines. Acceptance comes from getting to know yourself.

- Pay attention to the world around you. Notice and respect the life force in its many shapes and sizes. Be aware of your connection with all of life.

- Mindfulness is just being aware. It brings you into the moment, making life a wonderful and continually unfolding adventure.

Meditation in the World

One of the criticisms sometimes leveled at people who meditate is that they are wasting precious time being inactive when they could be engaged in activities like ending homelessness or poverty. However, meditation does not imply a withdrawal from action. Quite the contrary — it often stimulates even more active involvement in such service. Meditation teaches you how to be engaged, aware, and to participate in the world around you; therefore the suffering experienced by others is harder to ignore. It helps you to develop compassion and friendliness toward everyone, so your response is invariably to offer help in whatever way is appropriate for that situation.

Compassion for others is at the center of religious belief.

Meditation is not about creating a fantasy world where everyone loves everyone else and nothing wrong happens. It is about living in the real world and dealing with real issues with as much compassion, understanding, generosity, and care as you can. When you recognize that we all deserve to be loved and have the ability to love, then you can find ways to be of use wherever there is suffering.

In the Loving Kindness meditation practice, you extend a feeling of friendliness to all beings equally; in the same way, you can extend your service and generosity to everyone in the world. This may take the form of becoming a hospital or prison volunteer, or picking up trash while you are out for a walk, or sponsoring a child in an impoverished country, as much as it may mean building homes for the homeless, mediating for peace, or staffing a retreat center.

Many people travel to faraway countries to help fight the poverty there, but, in so doing, they can easily forget the poverty and great neediness on their own doorstep. Wherever you are, you can be of service to others. You do not need to be surrounded by hardship in order to practice generosity.

The saying: *Practice spontaneous acts of beauty and random acts of kindness* expresses how service is a natural response to life – you simply give of yourself in each moment. Try putting money in someone's parking meter before they get a ticket, helping an elderly person with their shopping, or giving someone who is cold a warm jacket to wear. Although you may not do this so that you will feel better, it is unquestionably a powerful feeling when you go beyond thinking only of yourself. Practicing generosity – especially giving a smile – will bring you the greatest joy.

Leaving the world a better place than you found it is what happens when meditation is brought into the world.

Caring for others brings a deep sense of fulfillment.

Nature Walk

Experience your oneness with all life by getting in touch with nature.

How often do you take time for a walk in nature? Not a walk for a certain reason like exercise, or to think something through, or in order to get somewhere, but a walk just for the joy of walking, to experience the beauty of being in motion and in nature — and for no other reason. It is the most precious gift you can give yourself. It puts you in immediate contact with the world around you and the other creatures who share this world with you. Make it a meditation, an expression of gratitude, of appreciation, of discovery. Walk for as long as you like.

◉ Whether in a city park, through a wood, along an old canal — there is always somewhere you can go that is full of nature. Walk slowly and gently. Be aware of walking. And be aware of the colors and the shapes, the smells and sounds that are all around you. Observe the birds and animals, the trees and the water. Notice how the flowers are growing, the different leaves on the trees, the trail left by a snail, or raindrops on a spider's web.

◉ Open yourself to the beauty of the natural world. If it is raining, appreciate the water on your face — the wet, cold, gentleness — and how this rain is nourishing the earth and the plants. If it is windy, observe the power of the wind — a force that is beyond your control. It if is gray and cloudy, watch for the shift in colors that produces ever more subtle shades, and notice the softness of the air. Although we protect ourselves from nature with raincoats, boots, and hats, we also need nourishment from the earth, plants, sun, wind, and rain.

⦿ Make this a special time for just you and the natural world around you. If you are with someone else, try walking in silence together, at least for a while, so that your appreciation can deepen. It is very special when you can walk in silence with another person; you will find yourselves communicating in a new way.

Sharing a connection with the earth can strengthen your bonds with others.

Meditation in Movement

Moving meditation practices like yoga, and martial arts like t'ai chi, bring meditation into the body. Through them, body and mind merge, the mind dissolving into the movements themselves.

If you have ever been to China, and to a city park there at sunrise or sunset, you will have seen a wonderful sight — people silently practicing t'ai chi in the rays of the early morning sun. It is particularly beautiful because, within the movement, there is a great stillness, as if it is an outward expression of deeper tranquillity. T'ai chi is a slow-motion dance, a series of gentle and graceful movements, each connected to the next, and each with a specific meaning. It is practiced to develop balance, concentration, good health, and inner relaxation and stillness — which is meditation. The energy of the practitioner is focused approximately two inches below his navel, which is known as the *hara* or source of *chi* (life force). T'ai chi and other forms of martial arts, such as aikido, are best learned with a teacher.

Yoga is equally ancient as t'ai chi — both go back well over 2,000 years — and is also meditation in action. The word yoga literally means "to yoke or unite together": a uniting of body, mind, and spirit through movement and deep relaxation. Hatha yoga consists of a series of postures, or asanas, that encourage physical release through invigorating the body, balancing the nerves, and bringing psycho/emotional ease. The word asana means "seat," or a quiet state of being, and the postures are designed to help you to find your seat, or center of stillness.

Yoga means "joining" — dissolving all sense of separation.

The asanas are also designed to move you beyond your limitations. In each posture, you use the breath to release any resistance so that both body and mind can relax. The breath and the body work as one, opening and releasing, and discovering an inner spaciousness. As the body opens, so does the mind. On the next page are some simple stretching and breathing asanas you may wish to practice. Beyond these simple exercises, we suggest that you learn more in a yoga class, working under a teacher's guidance.

Walking is another form of movement meditation. Walking is usually done automatically – with no thought or awareness – but it is a simple and direct way to focus our attention on one thing. It does not matter whether you walk slowly or quickly, indoors or outdoors; what matters is your ability to pay attention. You simply observe each movement as you lift, move, and place your foot on the ground, while also noting your breath. Keeping the eyes lowered to avoid distraction, enter into your own stillness as you raise and put down each foot. See page 86 for more instructions.

T'ai chi, the name of a system of slow movements, literally translates as "universal energy."

Stretch and Breathe Postures

These are basic yoga stretches loosen the body; they should be done gently and without strain.

STANDING POSE

This is a simple pose to align your body. Stand upright, feet a few inches apart, arms by your sides, and eyes closed. Spend a few moments standing and breathing and finding your balance.

Now imagine there is a string attached to the top of your head that is very slowly pulling you upward, lengthening your body. As it lifts you, your stomach comes in, your chest opens, your shoulders fall back, and your spine lengthens. Keep breathing and feel your body lengthening from your feet to your head.

Then very slowly the string relaxes, and your body returns to its normal position. Take a deep breath.

HEAVEN POSE

Standing upright, with your feet a foot apart, your eyes open and focused on the wall opposite you, stretch your arms up above your head, fingers pointing to the sky, head facing forward.

As you stretch upward, lift yourself up onto your toes. Keep breathing and stay focused in order to keep your balance. Feel the stretch all the way up your body, from the tips of your fingers, through your spine, and down your toes.

Stay here as long as you like, then slowly come back down and let your arms rest, releasing tension from your muscles. Repeat as desired.

STANDING POSE

HEAVEN POSE

FORWARD BEND

Standing upright, stretch your arms above your head. Then, bending from the waist, slowly bend forward, gently lengthening your spine, head going last, until you are as far downward as feels comfortable. If you can, let your hands rest on the floor; then slowly let your head drop down. With each *out* breath, feel your spine softening and releasing. When you are ready, breathe in as you gently uncurl your spine, eventually coming back to an upright pose, arms above your head. Continue moving backward, gently arching your spine, and then, on an *in* breath, return to your normal posture and relax.

FORWARD BEND

SUN BREATH

The following three movements flow together with the breath, which is one continuous, deep *in* breath. Practice the positions first, then add the breathing.

- Stand with your feet slightly apart, hands by your sides, palms facing backward.
- Breathe deeply into your abdomen while stretching your arms out to your sides.
- Continue the breath, filling your chest with air, while bringing your hands together at your heart in prayer position.
- Continue breathing into the upper part of your chest, while lifting your stretched arms up above your head, fingers pointing upward. Pause as you gaze heavenward.
- Exhale by blowing out through your mouth as you stretch your arms out to your sides and downward, as if outlining the sun. Then take a breath.
- Repeat this three times. Do it slowly and gently.

Walking Meditation

The practice of Walking Meditation was developed in the traditional teachings to balance periods of sitting meditation. If you sit for too long, your body will naturally become stiff, so, during long periods of practice, sitting was alternated with walking. But this is also a wonderful practice to do at any time. Walking Meditation enables you to become aware of something you do automatically; normally you just walk while you think or talk at the same time. Now you are purposefully not going anywhere or doing anything other than walking. This is meditation in action — you maintain awareness and concentration while also moving.

You can practice Walking Meditation indoors or outdoors, in bare feet or in shoes. You can walk in one continuous line, or between two stationary points about 30 paces apart, such as two trees. Walk from one point to the next, stop for a few moments, then turn and walk back. Usually this practice is done quite slowly, the idea being to completely focus your awareness on the movement of the body while being aware of the rhythm of your breath. However, if your body needs energizing, then start with a few minutes of vigorous but mindful walking, before slowing down to a more gentle pace.

This should be practiced for 15–20 minutes.

- Start by standing still. Your hands should be gently clasped at the front or back, rather than swinging loose, since this will keep your shoulders relaxed. Your head should be facing forward, and your eyes open but only looking at the ground three to five feet in front of you. Obviously you need to see where you are going, but it is important not to become distracted by looking at everything going on around you.

Let the body move slowly and with awareness.

- As you slowly walk, be aware of each movement as you lift, move, and place your foot. You can silently repeat, *lifting...moving...placing* with each step. Your body should be relaxed and at ease, your movements natural. You are just walking with awareness.

- As you relax into it, you will experience the flow and rhythm of the body and breath together, the lift and fall of each step. You will notice texture and temperature, weight and lightness. You are watching your walking and repeating the words in order to remain focused upon the movement.

When you finish, stand still for a few moments with your eyes closed, being aware of your breathing and your body. Enjoy the stillness.

After walking, stand still and focus on your breathing.

Lifestyle Changes

The more you meditate, the more you will find that you want to change your lifestyle and the way you live. Your lifestyle reflects the state of your mind and how you feel about yourself. Mindfulness makes you aware of this — of what you are eating, the quantity and type of food, as well as your behavior, habits, and preferences, and what needs to change in order to encourage greater growth. It is like bringing a breath of fresh air into a dusty room.

Your body instinctively knows which foods are good for it.

One of the main qualities that develops in the quiet and compassion of meditation is *ahimsa*, which means "harmlessness," the desire to no longer want to cause harm to yourself or anyone else.

You may find that you begin to eat less meat, partly because it seems too heavy and your body is happier on lighter food, and partly because you no longer want to eat animal products. Or you may find yourself carefully moving snails out of the way of oncoming cars, picking up trash in the street, or no longer participating in family arguments — all of which are expressions of practicing harmlessness in the world.

Applying harmlessness to yourself, you see how the food you eat has a direct effect upon your physical and psycho/emotional health. Being more aware, you will notice how certain foods make you feel tired and heavy, while others give you energy and vibrancy. Take more responsibility for your health by changing your diet so it corresponds with the changes taking place inside you. Spend a week eating fruit and vegetables, and notice how you feel. When you no longer want to harm your body, you will start to take greater care of it; getting more exercise or giving up unhealthy habits like smoking. Your relationship to yourself is deepening; you are becoming a friend to yourself, and this is shown in the way you begin to treat yourself.

Notice whether you fill every space of your day with something to do, from working and watching television to going out for a drink. Do you have spaces during which you can just be? As you meditate more, you may find that you are watching less television – perhaps reading or going for a walk instead – and that your inner world is becoming more entertaining than the outer one. Try going without television for a week and see how you feel and what you do with your time.

The level of clutter or chaos in your home and life also will become highlighted as you meditate more. The chaos outside you reflects the chaos in your mind, so, as you become clearer inside yourself, do not be surprised to find that you are becoming neater and more conscious of order. There is a natural order to all things, as in nature; when you respect this, you will find greater freedom in yourself.

Our diet is an expression of our caring for ourselves.

89

Personal Transformation

Meditation is a journey inward toward your spiritual center.

Meditation is a journey of self-discovery and transformation. Through it, you wake up to your intrinsic beauty, your true nature. You will find that you become a more loving individual, transforming fear into courage, selfishness into generosity, dislike into acceptance, aversion into compassion.

That may sound beyond your abilities, but take a few minutes to look back on how you were before you began to meditate, and note how you have already changed. Notice how much more at ease you are with yourself, even enjoying your own company, how you become less irritated and frustrated, are more willing to see another person's point of view, and how aware you have become of a world within you that you did not know existed.

A prisoner serving time in jail said that he always used to think that you just lived and died, and that was it. However, after twelve months of practicing meditation and yoga, he realized, "There's a hell of a lot more inside you than just the food that goes in!"

Change is the very nature of existence; nothing remains the same, always there is movement and growth. Just as the seasons change and the moon waxes and wanes, so do your thoughts and feelings come and go, your needs and desires change as you grow. To resist change is to resist life, sticking to old habits and thought patterns, separating yourself from the vibrancy all around you. To welcome change is to move with the natural flow of existence, where you discover a creative and

caring world in which you are an active participant, in touch with a continual source of inner peace.

Every journey begins with a single step. It takes great courage to step into a new place and do things you have never done before, but you have now taken that step. You may feel as if there are not that many signposts around and few familiar reference points, and you may only know one or two other people who are also going this way, but something inside you is saying "yes" – yes to making friends with yourself, yes to opening doors that have long been closed, yes to discovering the love in your heart, yes to ever-increasing joy and happiness.

Meditation lifts you out of your limited, self-centered world and shows you a bigger picture. It enables you to live with greater ease in a world full of confusion, and to have more room in your heart for those who are suffering. The greatest gift you can give to the world is such a change in yourself. It is through those individuals equipped with the ability to embrace this that the world can be improved, making it a saner, more loving place for us to live in.

Join with other individuals in the natural flow of existence.

Continuing to Practice

In this book, you have learned all you need to know in order to practice meditation. The only thing this book can't give you is experience. For this, you will have to practice, either by yourself, with family or friends, or in a group.

Practicing alone is lovely. This time is for you, where you can be with yourself, quiet and undistracted. Most people who practice will meditate alone every day.

But it is also good to practice with others, at least now and then. If you can share meditation or quiet time with your family, it opens up a new way of communicating and being together. Sitting in silence can bring a deep sense of unity to everyone present. They may not want to join you, but suggest that you start with just ten minutes together so they do not feel too overwhelmed by the idea. You don't have to do anything special — just sit silently and watch your breath or repeat a simple mantra. Try doing this once a week to begin with, and watch what happens. Those who at first don't want to participate may soon realize that they are missing something.

The openness and support of group meditation can be a nourishing experience.

Meditating in a group is a very valuable experience. There is something profound that happens when a group of people, who may or may not know each other, come together to meditate. It forms a deep connection between them. Participating in a group offers community and a sense of support, as well as a sense of belonging that can be very enriching.

To find a group check your local bookstore, library, health-food store, or telephone directory for information. You will find various groups following different meditation traditions. Try them and trust your intuition. If you don't feel right in a particular group, don't go back to it. Find one you feel completely happy with.

The same applies to finding a teacher. It can be very helpful to have someone who can answer your questions and steer you through the many experiences that may arise. But it is important that you feel comfortable and trust him or her. You do not have to have a guru, so don't think you have to sign your life away, let alone give anyone large sums of money. Someone may tell you that his or her teacher is the best, but you must also feel at ease with that teacher, yourself, and with the practices being taught. Give yourself time to decide what feels right. Most of all, trust your inner guru to guide you, for meditation is essentially your own true nature, a coming home to yourself.

You have begun a wonderful journey. May you enjoy your travels on the path to a higher consciousness! Use a card from this pack each day to remind you of your inner wisdom and to keep your meditation alive under all circumstances.

Use a card a day to connect to your inner wisdom.

Biography

Eddie and Debbie Shapiro are internationally known authors and seminar leaders. Together they are the authors of:
Ultimate Relaxation (1999, Quadrille UK);
Meditation for Inner Peace
(1997, Piatkus UK, Crossing Press USA);
Clear Mind Open Heart
(1994, Piatkus UK, Crossing Press USA);
Out of Your Mind – The Only Place to Be!
(1992, Element UK and USA).

They are the editors of:
Voices From the Heart
(1998, Jeremy P. Tarcher USA, Rider UK) – a collection of interviews with the Dalai Lama, President Mikhail Gorbachev, Archbishop Desmond Tutu, Ram Dass, Stephen Levine, Kitaro, and others.

The Way Ahead (1992, Element UK and USA), foreword by Richard Gere, contributions from President Vaclav Havel, Paul McCartney, Yoko Ono, Prince Philip, Allan Ginsberg, etc.

Eddie Shapiro, from New York, won the New York City dance championships in 1962. He is an expert skier and scuba diver. In 1968, he trained as a Swami with Paramahamsa Satyananda at the Bihar School of Yoga in India.
He is the author of:
Inner Conscious Relaxation
(1990, Element UK and USA).

Debbie, from England, trained over twenty years ago in bodywork and body/mind therapy, in both England and the USA, and in Buddhist meditation with Tai Situ Rinpoche.
She is the author of:
Your Body Speaks Your Mind
(1996, Piatkus UK, Crossing Press USA);
The Bodymind Workbook
(1990, Element UK and USA);
and the co-author of *The Healer's Handbook*
(with Georgina Regan) (1988, Element);
and *The Metamorphic Technique*
(with Gaston Saint Pierre) (1982, Element).

The Shapiros have produced *Ocean of Bliss*, an Indian rock cassette, as well as a number of deep relaxation and meditation tapes (see opposite for details). They are inspired workshop leaders who often make presentations at international conferences, on TV, radio, and in the media.
They live in England.
Contact them at *www.channelhealth.net*.

Stephen Levine, author of *Who Dies*, says
"I hope that your work is reaching many.
It deserves it and so do they."

Dr. Bernie Siegel, author of bestseller
Love, Medicine and Miracles, says,
"Eddie and Debbie Shapiro are two warm, capable and caring individuals.
Their work makes our planet a safer and more loving place to be."

Dr. Lex Hixon, author of *Coming Home*, said,
"The wonderful Shapiros are a conduit of joy and spiritual energy that heals hearts on their subtle levels."

RELAXATION AND MEDITATION TAPES
BY EDDIE AND DEBBIE SHAPIRO

Samadhi *Witness Meditation* to become aware of self in relation to thoughts and feeling, and *Breath Awareness Meditation* to focus the mind in the rhythm of the breath. These two traditional meditation practices are aimed at stabilizing the mind, developing clarity, self-awareness and innate wisdom. These are the foundation for all other meditation practices.

Metta *Loving Kindness Meditaion* to dissolve emotional traumas and develop true compassion and loving kindness for both yourself and others, and *Forgiveness Meditation* to release feelings of revenge, pain, shame, or guilt, and allow mercy and healing to fill your heart.

Karuna *Loving Heart Meditation* to open to the abiding love in your heart that is your true nature, and *Heart-centered Inner Conscious Relaxation* to release unconscious emotional tension and develop an open and peaceful heart.

Samata *Inner Conscious Relaxation* to release unconscious levels of stress, clear the mind of deep-rooted fears and tension, discovering a lasting peace and innate joy. There are two versions of this traditional practice, essential for entering into a deeply peaceful state.

Chidakash *Chakra Meditation* to awaken your highest potential through the chakras with visualization, color, and sound, and *Five Element Visualization* to free areas of blocked energy and develop awareness of higher consciousness.

Anamaya *Inner Healing Visualization* leading you within yourself to communicate with your body and to gain guidance for healing, and *Bodymind Awareness Relaxation* to bring appreciation, healing, love, and ease to each part of your body.

Ananda Sagare Indian chanting of *kirtan* and *bhajan* with music by Satyam.

To order: contact Eddie and Debbie at *www.channelhealth.net,* or write to them, c/o Godsfield Press Ltd.